D0709356

HOW TO
BE A GREAT
M.C.

HOW TO
BE A GREAT
M.C.

OR
HOW TO BE MASTER
OF THE CEREMONIES
AND
NOT BE MASTERED
BY THE CEREMONIES

ALEX MAIR

Hurtig Publishers
Edmonton

Hurtig Publishers Ltd.
10560-105 Street
Edmonton, Alberta
Canada T5H 2W7

Canadian Cataloguing in Publication Data

Mair, Alex.
  How to be a great M.C.

ISBN 0-88830-289-4 (bound).

1. Public speaking.   2. Meetings.   3. Leadership.
I. Title.
PN4121.M34 1986   808.5'1   C85-091515-5

Printed and bound in Canada

To
Kathleen, Lory, and Sandy,
who spent their
character-building years
learning to cope with
their father

Contents

The *Gage Canadian Dictionary* defines a master of ceremonies as "a person in charge of a ceremony or entertainment who announces the successive events and makes sure that they take place in the proper order. *Abbrev.:* M.C."

CHAPTER I

We've All Been There

Someday a perceptive scriptwriter is going to produce the screenplay for the funniest film the world has ever seen, and it will tell the story of the reception that didn't quite work.

The opening scene will be set in the dining room of a hotel, and you will be able to tell from the faces in the crowd that there is an element of confusion in the air. Eventually the viewers will come to realize that this is a wedding reception, but at this stage it's anyone's guess because there is a distinguished-looking couple, she in an evening gown and he in a tuxedo, asking people what time the piano recital is due to get under way.

The dining-room manager's voice carries across the room as he shouts, "What do you mean, a hundred and sixteen? You told me that there would be ninety-six maximum, counting the head table."

Uncle Floyd is over at the bar having a drink to calm himself. One more drink and Uncle Floyd will be so calm that he will make a sphinx look fidgety.

A wee man in a kilt, with firey eye and breath to match, gazes at the mixed gathering around him and is heard to say, "When did they start letting the lassies attend a Burns Supper?"

Over near the door, an unidentified guest is telling three others that he just heard that on their way to the photographer's studio, the bride and groom ran into the rear end of a garbage truck and the groom has been charged with causing a disturbance after trying to convince the truck driver that he shouldn't use language like that in front of the groom's new wife.

"How far away is the Bide-A-Wee Motel?" asks the bride's brother. On being advised that it is thirty-six miles past the city limits on the other side of town, he says by way of explanation, "The fellow who is proposing the toast to the bride just phoned from there. The transmission fell out of his car and he's got traffic on the freeway jammed up for a mile and a half."

An out-of-town guest whose contact lenses are back in his hotel room is peering into the eyes of the mother of the bride and saying, "Are you sure you were never the yoga lady on public television?"

The father of the bride, watching the bartender's magic fingers move at lightning speed, is heard to murmur, "Doesn't anyone drink coffee any more?"

The maitre d' is looking around for someone in authority so he can tell them to get the show on the road because the dinners are getting cold and the banquet permit runs out in an hour and a half.

The host, in an attempt to restore order, tries to make an announcement over the sound system. He finds that the microphone isn't working. The sound system magically comes to life as the host, holding the microphone two inches from his lips and using language usually reserved for the training of mules, comments on the mental capabilities and the questionable parental origins of the fellow who hooked up the sound system in the first place.

At this point the bride and groom arrive and the main action of the film gets under way. Like all great comedies, this one has sad undertones. It is supposed to be a happy occasion, but you can just feel that something else is about to go wrong.

This film should have great appeal because there are enough grains of truth in it to strike a familiar chord in the mind of every viewer.

This is a circus crying out for a ringmaster, someone who will ensure that all the things that *should* happen *do* happen. This affair needs someone to be in charge, someone who will master the ceremonies, not be mastered by them.

Just to make sure that the producers of this film can't find further inspiration at a function in which you are involved, let's consider this master or mistress of ceremonies. Let's talk about who he or she is, where they are found, and how they can go about doing the best possible job of making an event a success.

CHAPTER II

Why Have an M.C.?

Remember what the *Gage Canadian Dictionary* had to say about the rôle of a master or mistress of ceremonies: "a person in charge of a ceremony or entertainment who announces the successive events and makes sure that they take place in the proper order."

In one sense an orchestra conductor is an M.C. He presides over the entertainment and, as he points with his baton to each soloist in turn, he introduces the performers. The host of a television talk show is an M.C. in another sense. On the television program the host introduces the guests, making them sound interesting and exciting. The host keeps things moving, making sure that each event happens at the right time and seeing that all the pieces of business that come together to make up the program are introduced and dealt with in a suitable manner.

You wouldn't think of turning an orchestra loose to perform without a conductor. You wouldn't consider presenting a talk show on television without a host. When it comes to guiding a banquet, a reception, or any other public or formal function, an M.C. is just as important as a conductor is to an orchestra and a host is to a talk show.

Consider the wide range of events that involve a master or mistress of ceremonies:

- a wedding reception
- a graduation exercise

- an awards ceremony
- a dinner meeting involving some business and a speaker
- an evening honouring an individual
- a company dinner and dance
- a long-service presentation to a staff member
- a seasonal party
- any social or business function that will run more smoothly with a firm, informed hand on the tiller and an eye on the clock

There are very few limits to the nature or size of a function that involves someone acting as master or mistress of ceremonies. And just as no two conductors will lead an orchestra through the same piece of music in exactly the same way, so no two M.C.s will work their way through a program in exactly the same way. Pacing, timing, and emphasis may vary a little from one leader to another, whether that leader is an orchestra conductor or an M.C. Every conductor and M.C. will approach the musical score or the program in his or her own way and proceed from beginning to end in an orderly, interesting way, making the total experience as enjoyable as possible for those in attendance.

As conductor or M.C., you are expected to *lead* the entertainment, not to *be* the entertainment. Of course it doesn't hurt if you are entertaining while you are performing your duties, but your primary rôle is one of leadership.

And just as there is a wide range of functions calling for the services of a master or mistress of ceremonies, so too is there a wide range of sources from which a suitable M.C. may be chosen. The choice may be made from within the club or organization holding the event. At a wedding reception the choice may be made from among family friends or even from within the family itself. If this is a company function, the organizers may turn to someone from the firm for their choice.

When choosing someone to act as master or mistress of ceremonies, the organizers may have fixed in their minds a somewhat limited picture of the person they want. There is a good possibility that in their view a good M.C. is anyone who can stand behind the head table at a function and deliver clever one-line jokes to the audience as he swings from one item of business to the next. In their minds, the M.C. is witty, relaxed, able to put an audience at ease, and a pleasant speaker. Their ideal M.C. appears to be in complete command of all that is happening at all times.

That is not a bad picture to have and to hold. A little tricky to achieve, true, but it can become reality when the person chosen to act as M.C. has a clear concept of just what is expected, is suitably prepared for the event, and has the support of all those involved. The successful M.C. is not necessarily the person with a vast supply of snappy stories and a glib tongue.

There are any number of different kinds of functions that depend upon the guidance of an M.C. for their success, but there are only a few rules for the person who has agreed to be that master or mistress of ceremonies. Understanding and following these principles will enable the M.C. to carry off the responsibilities of the position with ease, grace, and efficiency.

If you have been approached to act as a master or mistress of ceremonies, you have been chosen to fill a very important, time-honoured position, and you will want to do the very best job possible. Whether your job as M.C. involves a wedding reception, the graduation exercises for your daughter's high-school class, a long-service dinner for your company's senior personnel, or any of the scores of other possibilities, there is a way to approach your responsibilities that enhances your chances of success.

You can be a successful M.C.

Let's talk about it.

CHAPTER III

In the Beginning

I f it does not start during the telephone call in which you were invited to act as M.C., the process of getting to work on the job you have agreed to perform should start fairly soon after that conversation.

You may feel that you are not clear about where your responsibilities begin and end. On talking to the other people involved, you probably will find that they are not very clear either. It may not be easy, but this is the time to establish what is expected of you and what you can expect from the others involved. Many of the points to be considered are not necessarily the responsibility of the M.C. but *somebody* has to look after them. In your newly-acquired rôle as M.C., you have two things to gain by bringing any questions forward: you will know that your concerns have been raised in the minds of the organizers, and you will have established the fact that you are interested in the total success of the function.

This is the time to talk, and the best aids to the process are a pot of coffee and a pad of paper. Arrange to meet with the people who have extended the invitation so you can discuss in detail what the event is all about and what rôle they expect you to play in it.

As the conversation progresses, you will probably find that you are asking questions for which there are no immediate answers. Don't let this be a cause for worry. The answers will appear in the days and weeks ahead. If they don't, ask the questions again. Your job as M.C. will run more smoothly if all of the details are looked after. You don't have to look after every point yourself, but somebody does. If you help the others involved to think clearly and cover all the fine points, you are going to make them look good, you are going to make yourself look good, and happiness will abound.

When you first sit down to talk, begin at the beginning. Make sure that you are clear as to the date, the time, and the place at which the function is to take place. These facts are usually clearly established, but it is just as well to write them down. It gives you the feeling that you have made a solid start on the planning process.

Any function, be it a wedding reception, a graduation exercise, or a social or business occasion, is made up of individual pieces of business that come together to form a single event. It is a good idea for the M.C. to have all of these separate items clearly in mind. You may not have to plan them, organize them, or worry about them, but you will be expected to introduce them. The more you know about what is expected to happen, the better you will handle your job.

Let us assume that the function is to start with a cocktail hour, then a dinner, followed by the business part of the event, which will take place after the dinner has been cleared away. As M.C. you should be aware of the bar arrangements for the cocktail hour. You don't have to make the arrangements, but you may be expected to announce to the guests what the hours of operation of the bar will be and what arrangements, if any, have been made for the purchase of drinks. Where is the bar to be located? Will there be a bartender on duty? If the guests must buy drink tickets, where will the tickets be available?

This is the sort of question that may be raised during your early conversations with the organizers. Having the answers will put you in a much better position to establish your credibility and get things off to a good start on the night of the event.

It will make everyone feel more comfortable if early in the

evening you explain to the guests what is happening and what the rules are going to be. If that explanation is delivered clearly and pleasantly, the event will be off to a good start. There will be no sense of confusion. There will be instead an unstated feeling on everyone's part that things are organized and someone is in charge.

By gathering your information early in the planning stage, you will achieve an important part of your rôle as M.C.: you will make the guests feel at ease on the night of the function. Don't be afraid to look into details. The M.C. may be expected to advise the assembled group that the meal is about to be served. If the dinner is being served in another area, the M.C. should know where all of these nice people are expected to go to eat and be prepared to tell them should the need arise.

It may seem to be a small point, but what are the wishes of the organizers with regard to grace before the meal? If they feel that this would be a nice touch, someone must arrange for an individual to ask the blessing. As M.C. you are the one who is expected to let the guests know what is happening. As soon as they have moved into the dining area, let them know that someone will be coming forward to ask the blessing. That gives the person saying grace a little warning that he or she is on deck and avoids embarrassment for guests who might otherwise find themselves chewing on their third bites from their crusty rolls when they suddenly find everyone around them bowing their heads for grace.

It is up to the organizers to decide which items they wish to include in their function, but as M.C. it will be up to you to see that everything that is *supposed* to happen *does* happen. As M.C. you have one basic objective for yourself during the occasion: *no surprises!* If you make sure at the planning stage that the details are being considered and that someone has been charged with looking after said details, you are more than half way to achieving your "no surprises" objective.

Working with the information you have gathered in your

preliminary conversations, give some thought to the sequence of these items and the duration of each. If you know what time you are planning to get the proceedings under way and what time you would like things to be finished, all you have to do is fit the separate pieces between those times. This may turn out to be a little trickier than you expect, but you can handle it.

Give some thought to time limitations that may be preset. Has someone set the hours for the bar's operation? Are there time limits imposed by the liquor licence? If the guests are to be fed, what time will the meal be served? Is there an orchestra coming, what time do the musicians expect to start playing, and how much time do they need to set up their equipment? Is there anyone at the function who has to catch an airplane or for any other reason leave at a particular time? Is there an hour by which the space must be vacated? These and many other points are not the direct responsibility of the M.C. but this is a good time to bring them up. In making sure that someone is aware of the fact that they need attention, you will have put yourself in a better position to do a good job.

All you are doing at this point is gathering information. A lot of the information won't be available until later, but at least the questions have been raised so that someone can start establishing the answers.

In the minds of many, your job may not seem to start until you stand up and take charge on the night of the function. But you know that your job really starts when you accept the invitation to act as M.C. If you keep yourself informed during the planning stage, you will feel more confident about the whole thing and you will do a better job on the big night.

Don't underestimate the importance of feeling confident.

In your early conversations with the organizers, have you:

- talked to the people who extended the invitation to act as M.C. and established what the function is all about and what rôle they expect you to play in it?
- established the time and place of the function?
- discussed such separate items as introduction of special guests, toasts, refreshments, and announcements?
- considered such time factors as predetermined hours of operation of a bar, when food will be ready, and when an orchestra will expect to start playing?

CHAPTER IV

Dealing with the People

From the moment you accept the invitation to act as M.C. until the function is finished, your job involves other people. Let us take a few minutes to discuss who these other people are, what they can do to make this event a success, and what you can do to help them.

At the top of your list of people with whom you will be working are the organizers of the whole thing. Their biggest contribution to your part in the program is their attention to all the little things that will come together to form the main event. Running a close second in importance is their willingness to keep you informed on all matters relating to the program. You can help them by asking questions related to the function as they arise in your mind, not saving them up until the last minute. You can help them by familiarizing yourself with the relevant information as it is assembled and by coming to the event prepared, willing, and anxious to do a good job.

The list of people with whom you will be dealing doesn't stop at the organizers. The names will vary from one function to another, but they could include musicians, entertainers, guests of honour, special speakers, head-table guests, and members of the hotel or dining-room staff who will be attending to the event. All of these people are working with you to achieve the same goal: an event that is a total success. This means that each item on your program takes place in an orderly, pleasant way, and that the guests leave with a smile, saying to themselves, "They didn't leave anything out." The others involved in the program can help to achieve this goal by making their contribution as effectively as they are able. You can help them do this by making sure that they know what their contribution to the program is expected to be, where they fit into that program, and at least approximately how long their contribution is expected to take.

All of this information is arrived at in consultation with the organizers, but it helps you as M.C. if you make sure that the information is not only gathered but *understood* by all of those involved.

You as M.C. are working towards the most important thing you can do for the other people on the program: you can see that they are properly introduced at the appropriate point in the program, that their contribution is aptly described, and that you are aware of any special circumstances or aids that may be involved in that contribution. It is a mutually supportive thing. If you help them to do their job well, then they will have helped you to do your job well. All of this may sound simple enough, but it takes a blend of cooperation, consideration, and planning. The end result will make all the extra effort worthwhile.

Let's see how all of this might work in some situations.

For any function, you should make a list of the names of all the people who will be actively contributing to the program. In one of your early conversations with the organizers, take each name on that list and consider all of the questions that will have to be answered and dealt with before that person comes forward to add his or her bit to the event.

If there are to be entertainers on the program, someone must discuss with them at least briefly how they view their contributions. A singer, for example, may assume that the invitation to perform calls for more than one song. If you have planned on hearing just one number during the dessert course of the meal but the singer shows up with sheet music for three songs plus two more for encores, you might have a problem on your hands. It could be a *big* problem if time is limited. Does your singer wish to be accompanied by a pianist? If so, does the singer bring the accompanist? If the singer brings the accompanist, who provides the piano?

You will notice that one question may lead to another when you are at this stage. A piccolo player, you are safe in assuming, will arrive with his own piccolo. A piano player, on the other hand, is not going to arrive with a piano in the back of his or her car. This means that a piano must be provided, which isn't usually a big problem as long as you know about it in advance.

You might wish to discuss with the organizers the arrangements that have to be made for the entertainers. If a dinner is being served, are the entertainers considered guests, and if so, are they served dinner? And if they are having dinner, where should they be seated? The entertainment may be provided by friends or associates who are part of the function anyway, but quite often the performers are invited specially for their contribution to the program. The whole question of the handling of the contributors to the program calls for a touch of diplomacy, but if you talk about the situation at an early stage in the planning process, you can put out a lot of little fires before they have a chance to turn into a three-alarm nightmare.

In many instances a special speaker will play a part in the program. This may be someone who is proposing a toast, making a presentation, or delivering a particular address. The organizers will have approached the speaker and arranged for his or her presence, but there are a number of other points to be covered, points best looked after at an early planning session.

In some instances the speaker or speakers may be introduced by the M.C. That works fairly well and can be kept relatively informal if the occasion calls for informality. In other instances someone may be asked to undertake the task of introducing the speaker or speakers. Having the job done by an individual charged with nothing other than the introduction gives that introduction a little more status in the scheme of things. It helps the speech to stand out as a highlight of the proceedings.

If you are going to do the introducing, fine. Make arrangements to learn enough about the speaker to do a proper job of the introduction. If possible make this a personal contact, even if you have to settle for something as simple as a telephone conversation. If someone else is to do the introducing, that's fine too. But whether you do it, whether the person asked to perform the introduction does it, or whether someone from the organizing group does it, someone has to get in touch with the speaker. Gather a little biographical information. If the speaker does this sort of thing on a regular basis, there may be a prepared biographical sketch available that makes the preparation of the introduction much easier. Some speakers can provide you with what, in scholastic terms, is referred to as a *curriculum vitae.* That is a rather fancy name for a brief biographical resumé of a career.

While talking to the speaker, you can also determine whether there are any special mechanical or material aids involved in the presentation. You might also find out if he will be attending the function, or even coming to your city if travel is involved, with another person. People who are contributing to a program often appreciate an invitation being extended to the spouse. If they are arriving from out of town, where are they going to stay? Is someone meeting them when they arrive? Is someone going to ensure that they arrive at the function safely and on time?

All of these details are not necessarily the responsibility of the M.C., but they will affect the way you are able to do your job when you stand up and take charge.

In your conversations with and about the other people contributing to the program, don't be afraid to talk about time. Tactfully ask how long the singer expects to take. Discuss the length of the speaker's address. If the speaker is to be introduced by someone, discuss how long that introduction is going to take. Remember, you are avoiding sudden surprises, and the passage of time can be a real source of surprise when your program gets underway.

Talk to the organizers about special guests who may need an introduction. There may be additions to that list right up to the very last minute, so be prepared for new names.

When you are acting as M.C. and introducing people, it is always nice to know not just their names but the proper pronunciation of their names, where they are sitting, and how they fit into the group. You may have the name of the distinguished gentleman sitting there off to your right, but it adds a great deal to your introduction if you can add that he is the president of the company's west coast branch and is in town for the directors' meeting. That nice lady off to your left, the one you are about to introduce as the bride's aunt, becomes more interesting if you can add that she has flown in from Miami just to attend the wedding and that she hasn't seen the bride for eighteen years. When introducing special guests, it helps if you don't sound as though you are meeting them for the first time too. You can avoid that by finding out a little background information during your planning sessions and chatting with them, even briefly, before the actual introduction.

And when you are sorting out pronunciation problems, don't stop when you have made sure you have their names properly fixed in your mind. People from other parts of the country are very sensitive about the name of the place they call home. Make sure your geographical pronunciation is accurate before you stand and tackle the place-name out loud before an audience.

One last group of names on your people list should include some key personnel from the facility in which the function is being held. Perhaps not at an early planning stage, but at some time before you take charge of the event, make sure that you know a few of the management people and that they know who you are and what your rôle is to be. As M.C. you will be acting as a funnel for information. If there is an important telephone call for someone in the audience, that message will be brought to you for transmission to those concerned. If someone has left his car lights on in the parking lot, the management has to know that you are the M.C. and that you are the one to pass on the lucky licence number. The flow of information will be *through* you, the M.C. Questions will be asked *of* you too. While you may not have all the answers, you will at least know where to turn to get the answers.

You are the M.C. but the ceremonies will involve other people. The more you know about what those other people are expecting to do, when they are going to do it, and how long they plan to take doing it, the more smoothly your job and the event will run.

You want to avoid surprises. The more you know about what is expected of the other participants in the program, the more they know about what is expected of them, the fewer those surprises will be.

In your early dealings with the people, have you:

- established some form of regular contact with the organizers?
- compiled a list of other participants in the program?
- if possible, called on these other participants to discuss their participation, how they view it, and how long they will spend doing it?
- been given a list of special guests and where they fit into things?
- checked the pronunciation of all the names and titles involved?
- made a few biographical notes on those you will be expected to introduce?
- made some form of contact with the establishment providing the space?

CHAPTER V

For Want of a Nail

There is an old nursery rhyme that says something about, "For want of a nail, the shoe was lost. For want of a shoe, the horse was lost," and on and on until disaster strikes the entire kingdom. You aren't involved in a battle and disaster isn't going to strike, but it is still a good idea to check for loose nails.

By this point you will have gathered a lot of little pieces of information that, when assembled, will make up the detailed plan for your event. Since you started to gather your information early in the game, you don't feel any particular pressure from the clock or the calendar. And since you have been making notes as you progressed, you have your information down on paper so that it can't run away and get lost.

You are about to put those pieces together in some sort of order, but before you start there is one more area of concern that must be covered. This is the time to organize the equipment that will be needed when the event takes place and arrange who will look after it.

You might wish to consider the needs of a speaker first of all. Many speakers use a variety of mechanical and visual aids to assist them in presenting their messages. In the early conversations with the speaker, he should be asked if there is anything he might need, things such as slide projectors, overhead projectors, screens, tape recorders, or special microphones. Some speakers find it limiting to have to stand behind a lectern and use the microphone fastened to it. There are small clip-on type microphones which enable a speaker to move back and forth a bit and which contribute to a feeling of more relaxed personal contact with the audience.

If slides are going to be a part of the presentation, take time to make sure that a projector, the right kind of projector, is going to be set up and ready for use. Different styles of projectors take different types of slide holders. It helps if someone has made sure that all of the pieces of equipment are compatible before you turn off the room lights and get the keynote address under way. Screens can pose a problem as well. If there is a screen that is part of the permanent furniture in the room you are using, things will work out quite well. But if you have to set up a portable screen, you may be surprised to find how much room those three supporting legs can take and how difficult it is to position the thing so that everyone can see it.

Little things, true, but remember that loose horseshoe nail that caused all the trouble in the nursery rhyme. A little thought beforehand can forestall a great deal of stress later on.

If music is to be part of the program, consider the needs of the musicians. That piano we talked about earlier can turn into a monster if someone hasn't considered some of the problems it might cause. It is quite likely that a piano can be made available in most hotels and dining rooms, but this will have to be arranged in advance with the dining-room management and could involve an additional fee. Then there is the question of whether the piano has been tuned recently. A discreet advance check by someone with an ear for music could save an awkward moment when the pianist strikes the opening chord.

Having established that a piano is available, in tune, and will be in the dining room, you might want to think about just where in the dining room. A piano is a big piece of furniture, and it is heavy. You don't want to be pushing it into position as the guests stir restlessly in their chairs. You want the program to flow smoothly and quietly from one item to the next, and trundling a piano around a dining-room floor doesn't contribute a thing to that smooth flow. A singer and the piano accompanist should be easily seen by the guests, which means that the piano can't be stuck off in a dark corner somewhere. And when you are thinking piano, don't forget the piano *bench*. You would be surprised to learn how often the piano is positioned, opened, and all ready to be played, but the piano bench is back in the chair storage room covered with dust.

If you are having entertainment of any sort, someone should consider the problem of lighting. The room arrangements will be such that any head-table configuration will be nicely illuminated and a lectern for speakers will be bathed in light. But a piano, although positioned nicely at the front of the room, may be in a dark area, making it difficult for guests to see the performers and giving the pianist trouble in reading the music.

The people who are providing the space and the facilities have a few needs as well. Whether the organizers are going to be holding their event in a hotel, a dining room, or some other rented space, someone should discuss with the management *all* of the things that are going to be needed. Don't limit it to the obvious items such as the menu, the number attending, and the hours of operation. Make sure you have everything covered, from the piano bench to the portable screen.

All of this isn't the direct concern of the M.C., but it will help you to function effectively as M.C. if you know that these details have been covered. It is easier to make sure they have been attended to in advance than to think of something clever to say while someone runs around the hotel trying to find an extension cord so that a slide projector can be plugged in.

Another group of people who are going to have very definite needs at most functions are the photographers. No matter what the function, someone is going to want to take pictures. They are going to more than *want* to take pictures, they are going to *take* them. Commemorative photographs are part of it all. If you accept this as the way it's going to be, then you can consider the question of photographers and their equipment well in advance of the event and decide how best to keep things under control. By working with the photographers, you can do a great deal to ensure that the pictures are taken with a minimum of disruption but will still be a delight to the participants for years to come.

The photographers covering the event will fall into one of three categories:

- the professional photographer who has been hired to record the event
- media people who want to cover it as a story for press, radio, or television
- the amateur photographers, friends and family, who want to take their own pictures of it all

Let's consider the professional photographers first. Their *job* is to take pictures of the event. They have to come up with photographs that please the people who hired them. If they don't, their future in the business world is going to be short. Part of pleasing their client involves minimizing their intrusion into the event they are photographing.

You will find that they know their job, and that they are fast, efficient, and discreet. You will usually find that they have done their homework before they show up with their equipment. They will know how to get in, get their pictures, and then get on to their next assignments.

But despite the discreet professionalism of the photographers, popping flash attachments and special lighting set-ups can be distracting. Talk to the management of the hotel or dining room where the function is to be held. They have probably had the problem of accommodating photographers before, and they might be able to suggest one or two places within the building that lend themselves to photographic settings. They want their facility to look good, and they may suggest a corner of the foyer, the main entrance area, or even a small private room nearby that might be available. Your professional photographer will work more efficiently with a minimum of interruptions, and if he can get his equipment set up in advance, he is going to tie up the guests of honour for a minimum length of time.

If you are expecting the media to show interest, the troubles with distracting equipment and lighting are only part of the problem. Your photographer, the one who has been hired to cover the event, will adjust his schedule to suit yours. Newspapers, radio stations, and television crews have deadlines, and they will be inclined to expect *you* to do the adjusting to fit *their* tight schedules. Assuming that you don't mind the coverage and that you have some idea of when they plan to arrive, you can often make some arrangements with the management for a place where pictures, videotape shots, or interviews can be handled with a minimum of upset to everyone's plans. A few minutes set aside for the media people so that they can do their job gets them on their way with the story and pictures, and then you can get on with what the organizers had planned for their event. The media people will appreciate the fact that you recognized their needs and tried to help.

Quite apart from the professional photographers and media people who might be covering your function, the amateur photographers deserve a little consideration too. Everyone pokes fun at Aunt Sophie and her drugstore camera, but they all want prints when they find that Aunt Sophie was the only one who brought a camera to the family picnic. As M.C., you can give Aunt Sophie and anyone else who remembered to bring a camera a better opportunity to take pictures if you think about leaving a bit of time just for pictures in the plans for your event.

Whatever the event, you can help control the photographic situation by a move as simple as telling the photographers what is going to happen and when. At a wedding reception, you should mention that the bride and groom will be cutting the cake in a few minutes and that the happy couple would be pleased to pose for pictures. That gives everyone a chance to check their flash attachments and move into position in front of the head table. The bride and groom can pose, knife held over the cake, and the photographers can pop away with their flash attachments. It takes only a short time, and then you can thank the photographers and suggest that they move back so that everyone can see the bride and groom. You created an opportunity for pictures to be taken without stress, you asked the picture-takers to consider their fellow guests and allow them a clear view. That's one way of keeping a handle on the photography situation. Of course there will always be someone who wants a picture of the *actual* cake cutting. None of this posed stuff, thank you! In that case, you are back to using your own judgement again, and good luck.

If the function is honouring a graduate, a retiree, or some other individual or group, it still makes sense to provide an opportunity for the photographers to record it. If you give a little thought to how that opportunity is going to fit into the plans, taking into account the circumstances, you can usually find a way to solve everyone's problems with a minimum of ruffled feathers. Tell the photographers in advance that you are going to give them their chance and they will, for the most part, go along happily with your suggestions.

Personal video recorders are becoming more common with each passing month, and these units pose slightly different problems than those raised by a hand-held camera. To start with, video recorders are bulkier and can be relatively heavy. To solve the weight problem, the camera operator can set his machine on a tripod with the recording equipment in a separate case on the floor beneath the tripod. The trouble is that when all this is assembled, anyone sitting behind the camera operator is going to have a hard time seeing the action, particularly if the operator jumps up and peeks into the viewfinder when the camera is in operation. If you spot the people with video recorders before they get too much equipment set up, you might suggest that they pick a spot at the side of the seating area so they won't be blocking anyone's view. You want to be helpful to the operators, but you need them to be considerate of the other guests.

If all the video recorder operators want to plug into the same power outlet because they don't have battery packs, they have a problem. So do you if they overload the circuits, blow a fuse, and plunge the room into darkness. Diplomacy is the password, and diplomacy is best practised *before* the problems become serious.

This also may not be considered to be part of the responsibilities of the M.C., but it is your performance as M.C. that is going to be disrupted if the whole business of picture-taking gets out-of-hand. You owe it to yourself to make sure that someone has given a little thought to the photographers in the crowd and is prepared to accommodate them in some way or another.

If there are any special pieces of business that are part of the program, consideration of the needs of those involved in each piece of business can help things to run more easily when the program is under way. Are there to be any presentations during the function? Bouquets of flowers, engraved wall plaques, long-service certificates, diplomas, or any of a dozen other things to be presented may form part of the proceedings. Anything to be presented should be close at hand when the time for the presentation rolls around. When Old Charlie comes up to the lectern to receive his gold watch from the president, it's a good idea to have the gold watch, Old Charlie, and the president all there at the same time.

If diplomas are being presented, a separate table to hold those diplomas must be provided. If this is a graduation exercise, those diplomas had best be arranged in the order in which the graduands are going to march across the platform or there is going to be a great deal of rummaging going on when the ceremony is supposed to be running smoothly and swiftly.

What is just a horseshoe nail to someone else could turn into a problem for the M.C. if it isn't checked beforehand.

In organizing the equipment involved, have you:

- written down the information you have gathered up to now?
- discussed special equipment needs with the participants and ascertained who is to provide that equipment?
- considered the placement of such special equipment as slide projectors, screens, and pianos?
- considered how, when, and where you will accommodate the picture takers?
- arranged for comfortable availability of presentation items?

CHAPTER VI

Putting the Pieces Together

I t is now time to put the pieces together, and when you are finished you will be able to see just how this function is going to operate. What you are working on is a plan for the event. Some might call it a program, others an agenda. Call it what you will, what you are going to end up with is a list of things that you want to happen, arranged in the order in which you want them to happen.

Sit down with your notes, a pad of paper, and a pencil. List all the things that are going to make up the function. Don't worry about any particular order at this point, just make sure you have them all down on your list.

The list will vary depending on the kind of function that is being held. For a wedding reception you would list things such as:

- introduction of the parents of the bride and groom
- introduction of special guests
- reading of messages and telegrams
- musical solo
- toast to the bride
- reply to the toast to the bride
- cutting of the cake
- any other specific things requested by the people involved

If you were acting as M.C. at a presentation ceremony, your list would be quite different. It would include in part:

- greetings from the president
- introduction of out-of-town guests
- introduction of head-table guests
- toast to the presentation recipients
- reply to that toast by one of the recipients
- individual presentations
- closing remarks by the chairman

Since each function is unique, the program for each function will be unique. Your only real concern is that the program include all of the things that should be part of the event.

With your list prepared, go through it again and mark those things that you feel will be highlights of the event. At a wedding reception, the highlights would include the toast to the bride, the cutting of the cake, and possibly the throwing of the bride's bouquet.

Now you want to arrange all of the things on your original list in the order in which you want them to happen. Start with the highlights, saving one of the bigger ones for the end of the program. First impressions of anything are important, but the last impression carries just as much weight. Try to end your program on a high note, a positive note. People will remember that and like it.

Looking over your list you will realize, for example, that the reply to the toast to the bride must come after the toast itself and that perhaps the reading of the telegrams should come toward the end of the proceedings. You might choose to introduce the parents and the special guests first, if you are dealing with a wedding reception. Following those introductions you may choose to proceed with the meal, if one is to be served, and then turn to the toasts, wrapping it all up with a song from the soloist.

These are thoughts, not unwritten laws. There aren't any really hard and fast rules for the arrangement of your program;

you just want to come up with something that is logically ordered and pleasantly spaced for the maximum enjoyment of all concerned.

Now spend a little time with a clock. Consulting your list of those things that will be included in your program, write down the estimated length of time each item is expected to last. If you know what time you plan to start, you can add the total time for all the individual pieces of your program and that will tell you what time you will be finished. It won't be an exact time, of course, but at least you will know whether the whole thing is going to run past midnight, at which time the M.C. turns into a pumpkin.

The importance of your finishing time will vary a great deal, depending on what you have planned to happen after your formal program. If there has been an orchestra hired, it will expect to begin playing at a particular hour. The members of the orchestra may want a little time to set up their equipment. The dining-room staff may wish a little time to clear away the tables. This kind of thing adds a little more pressure to your time line than an evening that just allows for a little social mixing at the conclusion of the formal program.

Even if the program doesn't call for a meal or music, there will be limits within which your program is expected to run. The plan you have before you, with times attached, is going to tell you whether you can work it all into the time limits given. If it fits, you are smiling. If it doesn't, you are going to have to make some changes. The nice thing is that changes are much easier to make at the planning stage.

When you are fitting the pieces together and arranging them in the best order, remember that if your program involves a meal, there are some things that seem best fitted in before you eat and some things that seem best fitted in after you eat. And there some things that can take place *during* a meal if your time is getting a little crowded.

The introduction of special guests is best done early so everyone knows who they are. An after-dinner speaker, by definition, comes after dinner, even though he might wish he could get it over with early in the evening so he could enjoy the meal too.

Now that you are happy with the sequence of events, you should recognize three things:

- The preparation of the program may be done by someone within the organizing group and turned over to the M.C. for execution. If this is the case, the M.C. should become so familiar with the program that he *feels* as though he prepared it himself.
- Although the program is all arranged, the M.C. must be prepared to be a little flexible if circumstances suggest that a change or two be made.
- Even when the M.C. thinks the program is all arranged, he or she must be prepared for the unexpected.

It is more than likely that when it comes to putting the pieces together, the bit you have been most worried about is just what you will say when you stand up and start talking. As M.C. you are part talk-show host, part football quarterback, and part orchestra conductor. You have a powerful tool to work with: words. Let's look at those words and how best to use them.

On accepting the job of M.C., your first instinct will be to pick up a notebook and a ballpoint pen, telephone all your friends, and shout, "I'm going to be an M.C. Tell me your six best jokes." The image so many of us have of the successful M.C. is the person at the microphone behind the head table keeping the audience rolling with laughter. The trouble is that that's not the rôle of the M.C. That's the rôle of the after-dinner speaker. All the M.C. does is introduce the fellow.

That is oversimplifying, of course. The M.C. should be interesting to listen to, easy to hear, and entertaining. The M.C. isn't the whole show, though; the M.C. just runs the whole show.

If you feel you would like to have some witty one-liners to drop into your remarks, by all means gather a few together and build them into your program notes. The "Humour" shelf at your local bookstore holds a wide collection of so-called joke books that will be of some help, but don't limit yourself to the obvious joke-book sort of material. Your local library reference section will have more books on wise ways to say things than you will have time to read before your big night. As you browse through the paperbacks at the book store or the reference books at the library, watch for the ones that make you smile or think or laugh. What you find funny or provocative or interesting, you can usually make funny or provocative or interesting to someone else. Don't be afraid to tailor the material to your own style and your own needs.

You might be looking for some short pieces to use at a wedding reception. Thumbing through *The Ad-Libber's Handbook* by Robert Orben (New York: Doubleday, 1969), you find:

> May 10th: Today, in 1893, that famous old locomotive, the 999, went a record breaking 112½ miles an hour. To show you how times have changed, the kid next door backs out of the driveway faster than this.

For your purposes at a wedding reception, how about a little touch here and a little touch there until it becomes:

> It was on the tenth of May, 1893, that Old Number 999, one of the world's most famous locomotives, set a speed record of 112½ miles an hour. It was on the afternoon of (name the date) that (name the bridegroom) pulled into the parking lot at the church going faster than that, which gives you some idea of how anxious he was to get to the church on time.

After you have carefully assembled and rehearsed a number of these "ad-libs," give them the Three Ts Test. Check your stories for:

- Timing
- Taste
- Tact

The business of timing may catch you a little by surprise. We all think we know how long it takes to say something, but do we really know? That nice, bright introduction you have put together, the one designed to make the guest speaker sound like the most interesting person in the hemisphere, when you check it with your watch, takes three and a half minutes to read out loud. What is three and a half minutes to a listener? That's more time than the weather forecaster gets each night on the television news, and he has to outline the weather for the entire continent, tell you how hot it is locally, and estimate the chances of rain for the next seventy-two hours. Advertisers can extol the virtues of the world's leading soft drink in thirty seconds. Does your introduction really have to be seven times as long as that soft drink commercial?

Take off your wristwatch, the one with the sweep second hand, and listen to a radio newscast as you watch the dial. You will be amazed at how many stories last less than twenty seconds. Do the same thing with the television news, and again you will be surprised at how short many of the items actually are. Our ears are trained to listen to short, tightly-written items. The short snappers you drop into your remarks will be better appreciated and better understood if they are just that: short and snappy.

The second point in our Three Ts Test had to do with taste. Everything that you say should be inoffensive to all present. Someone on a late-night television show might refer to an often-married actress as the only woman in the world with her own drip-dry wedding gown, but don't crowd your luck with that kind of a story. The guests at your function will probably have varied views and experiences. There will be a segment of the audience that won't object to a rather raunchy one dropped in here and there, but there are others who won't appreciate it. Keep it in unobjectionable taste.

A yarn on the blue side is a little like a sardine-and-onion sandwich. It may seem fine as you enjoy it late in the evening, but it leaves a funny taste in your mouth when you wake up the next morning wishing you could take it back.

And then there is tact. The *Gage Canadian Dictionary* tells us that tact is "a keen sense of the right or fitting thing to say or do so as to avoid hurting someone's feelings; sensitivity in dealing with people." In an M.C., tact is that and a little bit more. An M.C. can use a touch of tact in many instances, smoothing out the flow of events and keeping everyone informed. Consider the verbal cues that you might drop into your remarks. "Thank you very much for that splendid solo, Miss Cartwright. And now, before Old Charlie proposes a toast to the absent members, a little light piano music from Trudy McKenzie." Eleven seconds, thirty words, and you have:

- thanked the previous performer
- introduced the next one
- alerted Old Charlie so that he can tense up because he's next

The tactful part was the message to Old Charlie. You know that Charlie is a little hard of hearing and he's sitting in the far corner of the room. Those sitting with Charlie will help him to gather his bits and pieces together so that he is ready when called upon after the pianist has finished her solo.

You may want to back up a little and do Trudy McKenzie more justice with a longer introduction. That would be particularly appropriate if you've caught her by surprise and she isn't quite ready. If you glance over to the piano and see Trudy

49

frantically looking for the right piece of sheet music, you can relieve a lot of the pressure on her and fill that void of silence that could come between the end of your introduction and her first chord. Perhaps you can mention a little more about her training, her special concerts, and any outstanding or well-known teachers she may have had. This presumes, of course, that you have talked with Trudy during your planning stage and written a few of these things down.

But now, as you glance down, you see Trudy smiling up at you, her fingers poised over the keys. All you have to say is, "Ladies and gentlemen, Miss Trudy McKenzie and Johann Sebastian Bach's 'Fugue in G, the Little Fugue'."

Of course if Trudy were planning to play "Pale Hands I Love Beside the Shalimar," you both would be in trouble. With all the planning you have done, that sort of thing isn't likely to happen. But if it does, it's not the end of the world. Discreet, polite corrections are the order of the day. Don't make a big thing out of a small error.

When you sum it all up, familiarity with your program and the people in it will be your passport to a relaxed, poised, and competent performance in your rôle as M.C.

There is just one more piece to put together before you are all done, and that piece is yourself and the way you look. A wise choice of clothes can make a great deal of difference to the way you feel as well as the way you look when you are busy doing your job. When it comes to the clothes you are going to wear, it pays to give the matter a little thought before the big event. Once you have sorted out what you are going to wear, you can check to see whether a trip to the dry cleaner is necessary, whether there are any loose buttons that need replacing, or whether there is a long white thread hanging down the back of your jacket.

There are two broad rules that you should keep in mind when you are trying to decide what to wear:

- You should wear clothes that are appropriate to the occasion.
- When you are choosing your clothes, think cool.

A little thought given to the nature of the occasion will tell you what is appropriate. You want to be comfortable but comfort comes not just from the fit of the clothes, it comes from knowing that you have chosen the right clothes for the occasion. Having made your choice of outfit and made sure that it is ready to go, put it right out of your mind. When you are getting ready to leave for the function, you want to get dressed, check your hair in the mirror, and go. You don't want to spend the evening worrying about your tight shoes or whether you should have worn the black and white striped outfit. You will have enough on your mind without worrying about your clothes.

One last thought to keep in mind when you are making your choice of what to wear: most of the dining rooms and meeting rooms of the nation are well-lit and well-heated. You can usually count on the fact that the room is going to be warm, so choose clothes that are reasonably loose and reasonably light in weight. You want to stay cool inwardly and outwardly during the evening. The right wardrobe choice can help on both counts.

A successful event, like a jigsaw puzzle, is made up of a number of individual pieces. When you look at a jigsaw puzzle, you always notice the piece that's missing, never all of the pieces in place. This is a good time to consider all of the pieces that will come together to form your event, pieces ranging from your agenda and notes right down to your choice of clothes and your willingness to accept the unexpected if it should arise. When all of the pieces come together the way they should, you will be happy with the result, whether it's a puzzle or a party.

In compiling your agenda, have you:

- listed all the separate pieces of business that will come together to form the event?
- marked those items that should be considered highlights?
- arranged all the pieces in the order in which you want them to happen?
- checked the length of time each item is expected to take?
- calculated the length of time the whole program should take?
- prepared some personal notes so that you can make relevant, interesting comments as you move from item to item throughout the program?
- considered your comments from the point of view of timing, taste, and tact?
- sorted out your wardrobe for the event, remembering to keep it appropriate and cool?

CHAPTER VII

This Thing Called Protocol

Suggesting that you follow the rules of protocol at your function is a lot like asking someone to take minutes at a meeting. Suddenly everyone becomes very serious and all the fun goes out of it. But just as minutes help to keep track of what was discussed at a meeting and what actions are to be taken, so does a touch of protocol bring a little social order and sense of control to the function at which you are acting as M.C.

The *Random House Dictionary of the English Language* tells us that protocol is "the customs and regulations dealing with diplomatic formality, precedence, and etiquette." As far as an M.C. is concerned, protocol could perhaps best be described as rules that put everyone at ease and allow them to enjoy themselves to the utmost because they know that the things that need doing are being done, and done in the proper way.

Many of the rules of protocol are not unlike the rules followed by a good host or hostess. They are designed to put the guests at ease, ensuring those guests that they will not be offended on political, religious, or social points. And just as the rules you follow when you are being a good host or hostess can be adjusted to suit a given situation, so too can the rules covered by the term "protocol." Remember that the rules are designed to set people at ease and enable a function to run smoothly. Rules too rigidly adhered to can create as much tension as no rules at all.

Investigating the guidelines established for protocol is a lot like peeling an onion. You take off a layer, thinking that you are down to the core of the matter, only to find underneath another layer that can certainly bring a tear to your eye. The placement of the flags behind the head table, for example, is governed by protocol, and there may be someone in the audience who spots an error in a flag's position. This brings to mind a strange aspect of protocol: when you are right, nobody notices, and when you are wrong, nobody lets you forget.

What we are attempting to do here is to establish some guidelines for the average M.C. in an average situation, guidelines that will help the M.C. to follow through the function a path that will put everyone at ease and instill a feeling of confidence in the way things are being handled. Two axioms will help: you should follow the dictates of common sense, and you should follow the dictates of good taste.

Let's consider the problem of people and protocol first of all. If you find yourself with a room full of dignitaries, each of whom would like to be recognized, where do you start and where do you stop? If the mayor and the fire chief are both in attendance, do you introduce both of them, and if so, which one first?

When it comes to consideration of introducing dignitaries and special guests who are in attendance and where those introductions are to be fitted, pause for a moment and ask yourself a very basic question: who are the guests of honour? At a wedding reception, they are the bride and groom. At a graduation ceremony, they are the successful students. At a retirement dinner, they are the employees who have completed their service to the firm. The guests of honour are the ones to whom tribute is being paid. In planning your introductions, make sure that nothing distracts attention from the tribute being paid to the guests of honour. You will accomplish that by giving those introductions and special tributes a place in the scheme of things, a place that is separate, distinct, and timed so that they are presented as a highlight in the program.

In due course you will turn to the job of making verbal recognition of the presence of the mayor, the fire chief, the judge, the minister, or any other special guests. When you come to this portion of your program, you will find again that there are rules that you should keep in mind when you are bringing some order and sequence to these introductions.

When you are opening gifts, it is always a nice idea to save the best for the last. Do the same thing with your introductions. Start with the more junior people who are to be recognized and work your way up to the most senior.

Elected officials, from a protocol point of view, are held to be more senior than appointed officials. If you have a mix of elected officials in that they represent various levels of government, start with the junior governmental level and work your way up to the most senior. Your local municipal government would be the most junior, the federal government the most senior.

If you have any members of the armed forces whom you wish to introduce, remember that the navy is considered the senior service. In order of seniority among the armed forces, the army follows the navy, and the air force, being the new kid on the block, follows the army. In your introductions, work your way from junior to senior service.

If you happen to have the mayor in your audience as well as the fire chief, remember that the mayor represents the city and all the elected and appointed officials working for the city. When you introduce the mayor, you are recognizing him as the head of the whole municipal organization, so you don't have to introduce any other civic officials because the mayor represents them all.

There is a nice, comfortable rule to which you can turn if the whole thing seems to be growing too complicated or if your memory fails you: turn to the alphabet. Arrange things in alphabetical order and let it go at that.

Keep in mind that protocol is about half courtesy and half common sense. Adhering to protocol is a way of showing respect for your guests of honour and all your other guests, respect which touches upon their accomplishments, their political, cultural, or professional achievements, and their religious beliefs. Whether you call it protocol, whether you call it a set of rules, or whether you call it a series of pretty good ideas, it makes a great deal of sense as a way to approach some of your problems as M.C. Consider the seating arrangements at a head table, for example.

The purpose of the head table is to provide a place apart at which distinguished guests of honour or special participants in the program can be seated, served, and recognized with ease. The term "head table" doesn't necessarily mean a long table on a raised platform behind which sit a group of people who tend to feel a bit self-conscious throughout the entire meal. A "head table" could consist of a group of smaller tables at the regular floor level around which would sit the "head-table" guests. In that sense, "head table" is a seating area, not a specific furniture arrangement.

Having said that, and for purposes of ease in description, let's imagine that we are talking about a head table in a more formal sense, a long table across the front of the room, with a lectern and a microphone in the middle of it.

At many functions, the president of the club or organization acts as the M.C. Rather than confuse things, let us use the term M.C. to indicate the person who is managing the proceedings, realizing that the M.C. may very well have another title in the overall scheme of things. The M.C. should sit at the centre of the head table. He or she will be the one who will be up on his or her feet directing things and so will need easy access to the lectern.

Seated to the right of the M.C. should be the guest of honour. This may be the guest speaker, but the two aren't necessarily the same person. If you have a guest speaker in addition to the guest of honour, by all means seat the speaker at the head table, but not right next to the M.C. That chair is for the guest of honour.

Next to the guest of honour seat the spouse of the M.C. Husbands and wives are seated somewhere other than right next to their spouses. It makes for more interesting conversation during the evening, or so it is claimed.

After you have established the place at which your guest of honour is to be seated, the rest of the seating arrangements may be adjusted to suit the particular circumstances of the function. Just remember that it is customary to alternate between male and female guests and that a husband and wife should not be seated next to each other.

Depending on the type of function you are chairing, you might find a long list of people who feel that they deserve a place at the head table. You may have to gently dissuade some. It isn't necessary to find places at the head table for all the members of a committee, for all the members on the board of directors, for all the officers of the company. After the M.C., head-table guests are limited to guests of honour, special speakers, presidents, possibly a vice-president, and in some cases key officers within an organization. Those chosen to sit at the head table will be selected by the organizing group with whom you are working, but as M.C. you should be aware of the principles of protocol so that you are more comfortable in your rôle.

Don't be frightened by the word "protocol." The whole idea is to do things in a way that minimizes or eliminates moments of embarrassment or awkwardness.

Protocol is an ever-changing thing. For the most part, protocol is best considered as a set of guidelines rather than a rigidly-imposed law. As an example of the changing standards in protocol, remember that in some parts of the world it was considered improper for guests at a dinner or banquet to smoke until after someone had proposed a toast to the Queen. There may be spots on the globe where that rule of protocol is still adhered to, but they are harder to find with each passing year. Protocol tends to become less rigid with the passage of time, but it still merits consideration by all of those involved in the planning and presentation of any kind of function.

We said earlier that there are two axioms to keep in mind: you should follow the dictates of good taste, and you should follow the dictates of common sense.

Common sense would dictate that if there are elderly people in the audience, they should be seated and served in a location that minimizes any difficulties they might have in moving about. If you have a guest who is confined to a wheelchair, make sure the space between the tables is wide enough to enable him to manoeuvre his chair into position with a minimum of inconvenience. In some instances, seniors find that their eyesight and hearing are not what they once were. Take this into account when you are sorting out the seating arrangements. They will enjoy the function more if they don't have to strain to see and hear what is going on.

The whole question of seating is one that the organizers might consider at some length. The seating arrangement at a head table may be handled nicely through the use of place cards. Once the decision has been made as to who will be seated at the head table, it is a simple matter to put the names of the head-table guests on small cards and arrange them in front of the chairs at the head table. If the head-table party is to move into the dining room as a group, they could be gathered in a convenient spot outside the dining room and arranged in the order in which they will be sitting. Then they can move into the dining room, walk across the platform upon which the head table is arranged, stand behind their chairs, and then sit down in unison. This presents an appearance of calm and order and avoids creating the appearance of a group of people rehearsing for a game of musical chairs.

Tables reserved for special guests, seniors, or others should be clearly marked as reserved, and the guests you wish to be seated at those tables should be quietly informed that those tables have been set aside for their use.

Protocol is supposed to bring a sense of order to the proceedings, not be another source of concern. If you feel you would like to check a point of protocol or learn in more detail some of the fine points of protocol, your local library reference section is a good source of information, and many governmental bodies retain a protocol officer who may be called upon for a word of friendly advice.

In considering protocol, have you:

- looked over the program and considered any possible religious, political, or social considerations that should be shown respect?
- kept common sense and good taste in mind when seeking solutions to these problems?
- arranged your program so that the real guests of honour are highlighted?
- considered any other special guests you might wish to introduce, found an appropriate place in the program for these introductions, and arranged them in order so that the last to be introduced is the most senior?
- checked to see that the head-table seating is arranged along the principles of protocol, allowing for recognition and ease of operation during the function?
- considered the courtesies that can be extended to all of the guests, including the seniors and the physically disadvantaged?

CHAPTER VIII

Now Is the Hour

Like the tip of an iceberg, your performance as M.C. during the event is all that people really see of your job. It was probably the only part of the work involved that you were aware of before all of this began, and it is quite likely that it was the only part of the job that you were really worried about. How well the tip of the iceberg looks depends to a large extent on the nine-tenths of the iceberg that isn't visible.

The audience won't see the time and effort that have gone into gathering the people and the information that are going to make the function a success. They won't see the time and thought it has taken to arrange the sequence of events that are about to unfold as the program proceeds. They won't be aware of the thought that has been given to the timing and pacing of these events, and they won't see the level of cooperation and understanding that has been built up amongst the performers, the participants, the organizers, and yourself as M.C.

They won't see the time that has been taken to attend to details that range all the way from the light level on the pianist's sheet music to the proper pronunciation of the name of the home town of the fellow who is to introduce the guest speaker. They won't see the nine-tenths of your iceberg, they will only see the one-tenth that is an M.C. guiding them through a program with relaxed ease. They won't see those other nine-tenths, but they will sense them, whether they realize it or not. Without the attention that has been paid to the nine-tenths that are not visible, the one-tenth that is visible wouldn't look nearly as good.

But the hours of preparation are now behind you. The moment of truth has arrived, and in a few minutes you are going to have to stand up and be an M.C. There are probably only two rules to keep in mind:

- Relax, so that you are aware of what is happening around you.
- Remember that you are there to direct things, to see that they run smoothly.

As the group begins to gather for the function, wherever it may be held, it is a good idea to move about amongst the guests. This gives you an opportunity to mix with the group and to make sure that the key players have arrived and are ready.

If you should find that one of the participants in the program has yet to arrive and it is getting close to starting time, you may wish to delegate someone to do a little checking. Perhaps the guest is having trouble finding a parking spot. Perhaps he is in the building but can't find the right room. If you are really concerned, ask someone who will recognize the missing guest if they would mind checking to see if there is a problem. Don't go yourself. You will only get all hot and sticky racing around looking for the guest, who will probably arrive a minute after you tear out of the room to try to find him.

If it gets really serious, don't forget the telephone. A call to the missing guest's home or office will probably confirm that the missing one has left but was held up and made a late start. Knowing that the guest is on the way will usually ease your mind.

Watch the clock. As the crowd gathers, mixes, and talks, you may find that time passes a great deal more quickly than you realize. You have a timetable. If at all possible, stick to it. Fifteen minutes lost before you get under way can cause you trouble later on. One last check to make sure that all your players have arrived and are more or less in place, and you are ready to get things under way.

Let's consider a fairly typical event and follow it through from beginning to end. This will give you an idea of what you would be doing if this were the function at which you had agreed to be M.C. Recognizing that no two functions are exactly alike, perhaps we can discuss one type of event and use that as an example of the way things might happen.

Let's assume that you are to be M.C. at a wedding reception. For our purposes we will take the term "reception" to mean not just the formal receiving line but the dinner to follow and all of the pieces of business to be worked into the program, including the vocal solo by the bride's Aunt Clara.

After the guests have passed through the receiving line there is the meal, the toast to the bride, and the groom's response to that toast. The bride's mother and father are to be there as well as the groom's mother and father. You have met all these people, you know what they look like and the way they prefer to have their names pronounced. The best man has handed you half a dozen telegrams that were received during the day, and you know that you are to read them during the latter stages of the dinner. You have found a quiet corner, read through each telegram, and made sure there are no unpleasant surprises as to content, place of origin, or sender. You have checked the pronunciation of the strange place name on the one from the East, and you took the time to find out that the one signed Clark and June came from the bride's aunt and uncle who are holidaying in Hawaii and couldn't make it to the wedding. You have even pencilled that little bit of information in one corner of the telegram so you can mention it after you have read the telegram itself. Not everyone will know who Clark and June are and why they aren't at the wedding.

You have met the man proposing the toast to the bride. He is an old friend of the bride's family and he has told you that his toast, when checked seven times in front of the bathroom mirror, runs four and a half minutes. You are to introduce him, and you have long since learned, over a pot of coffee, enough about him to enable you to do a creditable job before the assembled guests.

Aunt Clara is in the ladies' room spraying her throat, and her accompanist has already checked the piano, found a little cushion that will make the piano bench the right height, and established that she will be able to read her music even if the room lights are turned down.

You have checked with the maitre d', the meal will be ready to serve on time, and word has just been telephoned to the front desk of the dining room that the bridal party has left the photographer's and will be at the reception in fifteen minutes.

The bridal party arrives, the receiving line is assembled, and the guests begin to file past. Eventually the last of the guests will have kissed the bride, shaken the groom's hand, talked briefly to the others in the line, and carried on into the dining room. The first of those through the reception line will have finished all of the olives, the celery, and the crusty rolls, and they will be waiting for you to take charge. It is time to get things under way.

With your program notes in front of you, switch on the microphone, put a big smile on your face, and welcome the group. You may not have a microphone, but a spoon rapped on the side of a water glass or empty coffee cup does a very effective job of attracting attention. Give them a moment to finish what they were talking about in their individual conversational circles, then if they haven't settled down, rap on your glass again and ask for their attention. You are in command, and it is best to have this point established right from the beginning.

You may choose to introduce yourself, explaining that you

are the M.C., and welcome them again in your own words. Don't be afraid to give them an outline of what is going to happen. It makes them feel more involved, and they'll like you for that.

It is about this point that you will realize how much your planning and preparation are going to pay off. There will be a warm feeling of confidence that stems from your awareness of what is happening and how firmly you have things under control.

Don't be afraid to exercise your own judgement. This doesn't mean that you should throw away your entire program, but be prepared to adjust it a little. Since no two functions are exactly the same and circumstances at any event will vary despite the most detailed planning, it is impossible to lay down hard and fast rules that will cover all circumstances. What you would like to have happen is a reasonably even flow of activity that leaves you and the guests feeling relaxed, entertained, informed, and comfortable.

While you were lining up your program, you will have kept in mind the principle that your guests of honour are the bride and groom and that the events in the program should support the honour you are extending to them.

The guests, having just come through the receiving line, have one more formal piece of business ahead of them, the toast to the bride. You may find that some people feel that a toast to the bride's mother is also a part of the formal wedding reception. Custom will vary from one group to another and with the passage of time. In some circles, for example, it is considered a nice touch to toast the bride *and* the groom. Toasts to the bride's parents and the groom's parents may also form a part of the program. These decisions will have been made with the organizers during the planning stage.

Let us assume that it has been decided that the toast to the bride will be proposed as soon as the guests are settled in the dining room and the head-table party is in place. As M.C., you would call upon the person proposing the toast to the bride and introduce him accordingly. The groom would reply to the toast to the bride, brief as that reply may be, and you could then invite the guests to be seated and proceed with the dinner.

Once you have settled the guests in their chairs, the dining-room staff can begin serving salads. This is the time to move quickly to the next item on the program. Does the program call for someone to say grace before the meal? Before the first fork is ever lifted, it would be a good idea to announce that you would like to call upon the Reverend John Smith to ask the blessing. Little verbal clues to your audience can save them the embarrassment of sitting too soon or polishing off their wine before all the toasts have been proposed. Don't be afraid to keep your audience posted on what's happening.

Before dinner may be a good time to introduce the head-table guests. It gives the rest of the guests something to look at and listen to while the salads are being served, and it is a nice way to get things under way. Again, verbal cues let everyone know what is expected of them. You can say, by way of starting the introductions, that you would like each member of the head-table party to stand as they are introduced and to please remain standing until all of the head table has been introduced. You can further ask the audience to withhold their applause until the last of the head-table guests have been introduced. When you have introduced the last person on your head-table list, a simple, "Ladies and gentlemen, your head table," does very nicely as a cue to your audience that you want them to applaud. When the applause has subsided, you can add a crisp, "Thank you very much, ladies and gentlemen. Now, enjoy your meal."

There is a point that you should consider when you are preparing and delivering the head-table introductions. There will likely be someone at the head table who will be playing a special rôle in the program later on. You, or someone else, will be introducing that individual more formally just prior to his or her big contribution to the proceedings, but don't ignore him or her during your introductions. Try something such as, "Next we have Mr. Jim Smith, who will be proposing a special toast later in the program. More about Jim by way of introduction at that time."

Another small point, but a helpful one from the audience's point of view, has to do with the introduction of spouses at the head table. It helps your listeners if you make some sort of association between the two people involved when you are introducing the spouse of someone who is either well-known to the group or who is going to be introduced at great length in a few minutes. Something along the lines of, "Next we have Mr. Roger Lancaster, husband of Mary Jean Lancaster, from whom we will be hearing later in our program." It helps people to match up faces and creates a stronger sense of familiarity with the head-table party.

At this point you are well launched into your program, and it is apparent that you are in charge of things. You have your sequence of events listed on your program notes in front of you, but to a certain extent it will be a matter of your personal judgement exactly when each event takes place. Keep things moving without the appearance of rushing things.

It is usually a good idea to let everyone enjoy the main course in peace. Get back to the business at hand before dessert, if you wish, but try to leave the main course for eat-up-and-talk time. Let them get their conversations out of their systems and then they'll be quiet when your program starts up again.

An exception to this rule could arise if you find that the dining-room staff are a little slow at getting the dinners out. It isn't the best procedure, but you may find, in the interest of time, that you have to get on with things before the last guest has been served his or her main course. Better that than having everyone else sitting around rattling coffee cups while the last few to be served finish their baked potatoes.

Your judgement comes into play again as the guests move on to the dessert course. This can be a low point in the scheme of things. The guests have enjoyed their meals and their conversations, but it's time to perk them up. You are well-advised to get things underway while dessert and coffee are being served. It can be a noisy time as dishes are rattled and serving staff move about the room, so don't try for anything too heavy. But there are items such as the introduction of out-of-town or special guests, the reading of telegrams, or special announcements that can be fitted in comfortably at this point.

Keep it moving but avoid any impression of haste.

With the meal behind you, you can return to the items on the program. The sequence of these items will have been sorted out during your planning sessions, but before you start on any of them try to wait until the dining-room staff have cleared the dishes. If there is anything else you can turn to while the last of the dishes rattle their way out of the room, do it.

Once the room is quiet, you can get on with the next high point on your program. Let's say that it is one of the special toasts. Tell the guests that the next item on the program will be, for example, a toast to the groom's parents. Proposing that toast, you tell them, will be Mr. Tom Brown, who has been a close and valued friend of the groom's family since the early years of their marriage and who has watched the groom grow from a freckled-faced toddler to the distinguished bridegroom they see tonight. Turning to where Mr. Brown is seated, you can say, "Ladies and gentlemen, Mr. Tom Brown." Mr. Brown rises, moves to the microphone, and proposes his toast.

You would, of course, put that introduction into your own

words, but remember to keep it brief. They want to hear the toast, not the introduction of the toast proposer.

Once that toast proposer stands up and starts to talk, there is precious little you can do about what he says or how long he takes to say it. If you are going to have any effect on this portion of the proceedings, it has to be done early in the planning stage. That's when, with tact and understanding, you can let the speaker know what is expected of him and roughly how long he will be expected to take doing it.

When the toast has been proposed and everyone is sitting down again, thank the proposer and turn to the next item of business. Your thanks to the toast proposer should be extended with grace, sincerity, and brevity, and the greatest of these is brevity. If the speaker has been humorous, there is a tendency to try to be funny in your response. Think about the host on a television talk show. If he has a comedian on his show, he never tries to top the comic. The host thanks the comic, tells him how funny he was and how much everyone enjoyed his performance, but *the host never tries to tell a joke*. It's all right for the M.C. to be entertaining while doing the job, but the M.C. is not the entertainment.

There will be other items on your program, items that were discussed during your planning sessions. Turn to them as they come up. The first thing you know, you'll be down to the last item and you'll be wondering how the time could have passed so quickly.

We haven't referred to any specific examples of the kind of notes you would take with you to the lectern for use as you work your way through the program. It is important that you prepare and use notes that make sense to you, notes to which you can refer with ease and which have lots of little reminders built into them so that you won't leave anything out. Don't be afraid to go into lots of detail when you are preparing these notes. You won't be sorry when the time comes to put them to work. There is nothing wrong with preparing program notes that say:

Item 19. TOAST TO THE PARENTS OF THE BRIDE AND GROOM

The M.C. will introduce Mr. Sam Wentworth, who will propose a toast to the parents of the bride and groom. Everyone except the parents of the bride and groom will stand for this toast. There will be no reply to the toast to the parents.

Copying machines being as accessible as they are these days, there is nothing wrong with making sure that the head-table party has copies of these detailed program notes. The parents will have been advised that they are to be toasted and that it isn't necessary for them to rise at any point or to say anything in reply. With a little verbal guidance from the M.C., everyone else will know what is happening and will respond in an appropriate way.

When you reach the end of the formal program, you will probably feel a great easing of the tension you will have been feeling to a certain extent all evening. If there has been an orchestra hired, you probably will have noticed them setting up as quietly as they could on the far side of the room. If there are tables to be cleared, you may want to announce that there will be a short break while the hotel staff clears the room in preparation for the dance to follow.

But for you, the hard part will be behind you and you will feel happy knowing that you have done a good job.

Before you get the event underway, have you:

- made sure you have your program notes with you?
- given yourself enough time to arrive a little early?
- moved about amongst the guests and checked to see if the other participants in the program have arrived?
- kept yourself aware of the time?
- walked around the room where the function is to take place and familiarized yourself with the placement of things?
- reminded yourself that all you have to do now is follow your program?

CHAPTER IX

What to Do If...

I t was the Scots poet Robert Burns who said, "The best-laid schemes o' mice an' men gang aft agley." That's a nice way of saying that no matter how much you plan, things don't always work out the way you had in mind. Robert Burns was talking to a mouse at the time, but he could very well have been speaking to an M.C. when he uttered those prophetic lines.

No matter how hard you try, no matter how much planning and preparation go into your job as M.C., there is always the chance that something will go wrong. Let's look at a few of the things that might upset your plans and consider how you might cope with them. Out of this will come the realization that no matter what crisis crops up, there is a way around it if you don't panic.

Let us assume that you are acting as M.C. at a banquet. You have planned a program that covers the entire evening. Now, let's pose a few problems that might crop up.

One of the situations we have already considered. *You have your program organized so that things get under way as soon as the meal is finished. But either the kitchen or the dining-room staff are very slow, the hands on the clock are whirling around at an alarming rate, and you realize that you are falling farther behind your schedule with every passing minute.* Don't panic!

A quick verbal check with those involved in the program, perhaps a word to the maitre d', and you can stand up and get your program underway. There may be movement of dining-room staff throughout the room, there may be the sound of dishes being rattled or coffee cups being filled. But there is nothing that says you can't start your program before the dinner is completely served if time dictates that you take this step.

In this situation you are working *around* the difficulty. Better to have a few distractions going on in the room than to keep everyone waiting until things settle down completely. Dining-room staff are trained to work quickly and quietly, they'll have their job done before you know it, and everyone will bless you for getting started with the business at hand.

Suppose, when you stand up to speak for the first time, you find that the microphone doesn't work? Don't panic!

Ask someone near you if they will contact a dining-room representative and report that the microphone isn't functioning. Having done that, check the on/off switch. Make sure the connecting wire is still fastened to the microphone. Follow the wire back to where it connects with the wall outlet and make sure that the connection is tight. By this time either you will have solved your problem or someone from the dining-room staff will be there to give you a hand. Sending for help with the audio system is like sending someone to phone a tow truck when your car won't start. The instant you know the tow truck is on the way, the car starts. Chances are the same thing will happen with your microphone, and if it doesn't you now have someone to solve the problem for you.

What do you do if, before your function starts, you realize that there aren't enough tables and chairs set out?

You or someone from the organizing group should get in touch with the maitre d' or some responsible person on the dining-room staff. Don't take the time to try to find out who miscounted. Just establish what you need in the way of extra seating and let them get at the business of setting it up. They know where the tables and chairs are kept and where they keep the extra knives and forks. If this leads to difficulties with regard to the number of meals that have been prepared, that's another problem. At least you have a little time to find a solution to that one. And if ten per cent of the guests dine on roast beef and the rest on broiled chicken, nobody is really going to remember in the morning, provided you handle it quietly and discreetly. If you must yell at someone, do it when the guests are all gone.

What happens if your guest speaker goes to the wrong address? Again, don't panic. There was an occasion when the guest speaker at a college graduation showed up at the right time but in the wrong part of town, and the problem was solved without too much stress.

The initial discussions with the speaker had taken place over dinner in the faculty dining room. During the dinner she had been briefed on the date and time of the event, the number of graduands in each course, the job placement record for each group, the total enrollment at the college, and the number of courses offered. It was a complete rundown of the relevant information except nobody thought to mention that the graduation exercises were to be held in an auditorium on the other side of town. It wasn't her fault that she showed up in the wrong place half an hour before things were to get under way in the right place.

Meanwhile on graduation day at the auditorium, the students were all lined up, the orchestra was working its way through the "Pomp and Circumstance Overture" for the third time, and the platform party was, with one exception, lined up and ready to march down the aisle. And what happened?

The platform party marched down the aisle on schedule, followed by the graduands. One person was delegated to find a telephone and attempt to find out what had happened to the guest speaker and then get word to the M.C. The appropriate chair on the stage was left vacant, and no particular mention was made of it during the introduction of the platform party.

One telephone call back to the college established that the guest of honour had arrived at the wrong location but that she was on her way to the right one. A note was passed discreetly to the M.C., easing his mind. The speakers earlier in the program, those bringing greetings from various levels of government, were encouraged to take a minute or two longer if they chose to do so.

The telephoner waited at the main door of the auditorium, met the guest speaker, and explained that although the program was underway, there was no immediate need to rush up onto the stage. They sat in the rotunda for a minute or two and talked until the distressed speaker had had a chance to get her pulse and respiration rate back to normal. The person who had met her then escorted her down the darkened side aisle of the auditorium. They sat in two vacant chairs on the aisle until the speaker then at the lectern finished his remarks, and then she quietly moved onto the stage and took her place with the platform party. A little tension in the air for a while, true, but the number of people affected was kept to a minimum, a solution was found, and it all worked out well in the end.

Suppose that the gentleman who was to introduce the guest speaker has been involved in a minor traffic accident. He's not hurt, but he is tied up at the scene of the accident and has telephoned to let you know that he won't make it in time to do his job, and his introduction notes are in his jacket pocket. What do you do?

For the M.C., there is always the ultimate solution. When all else fails, do it yourself.

You might leave your place at the head table while the main course is being served, seek out the guest speaker, and either pull up a chair at his side or kneel down and chat with him for a few minutes. Explain what has happened and tell him that you would like to make a few notes so that you can do the introducing. On the back of a menu, an old envelope, or any other piece of paper, jot down the answers to some key questions:

- Get his name right.
- Check his title (Doctor, Reverend, President, or whatever).

Then turn to some personal information that will make him of more interest to the audience.

- Married?
- Children?
- Born where?
- Lived where?
- Living now?
- Any special hobbies or interests?

That is about all you need under the circumstances. You are going to need about one minute's worth of material to do the job justice, and if you have answers to these questions, you're all set.

What do you do if there is a loud, disruptive noise when things should be quiet? Let's say that your guest speaker is far enough into his address to have gained the attention of the audience and settled them down. Then, somewhere in the room, a telephone rings. What do you do?

Find it and answer it as quickly as possible. Nobody can ignore a ringing telephone, so stop it ringing as quickly and as quietly as you can. A ringing telephone is a lot like a barking dog. It won't necessarily go away just because you try to ignore it.

And what if the disruptive noise is coming from a table at the back of the room, from a table at which the occupants have lingered a shade too long over the grape? Send someone to talk to them. Don't try to handle it from the head table or the lectern. Keep the disruption to a minimum, but try to snuff it out before it gets any worse. One person approaching the table and asking politely for their cooperation should do it, even if that person has to pull up a chair, sit down at the table, and with arms folded pay rapt attention to the speaker.

Extreme weather conditions interfere with the arrival of delegates to a three-day conference, and your entire program is built around the remarks to be given by a keynote speaker at the start of the conference. Your keynote speaker is to deliver his opening address during the evening session at the start of the conference, and the next morning the delegates, working in groups, are to begin discussing his remarks. Your keynote speaker has arrived, but a severe storm is interfering with the arrival of many of the delegates. It is likely that they will all be on hand in the morning, but only about half will be in attendance to hear the keynote address.

Let the speaker go ahead as planned. Let those in attendance listen to his address and make their notes. Be very nice to the keynote speaker and ask him if he could arrange to repeat his address the following morning, allowing for the fact that about half of the audience will have heard him the evening before. Most people who are asked to deliver an important address such as this are sufficiently familiar with their material that they are able to restructure a talk in such a way that it sounds reasonably fresh to people who have heard it before but still contains all the relevant material they wish to present. If you have a cooperative speaker, the keynote address can be rescheduled for the start of proceedings the following morning, you can trim and tailor some of the other pieces of business you had planned to deal with in the morning, and before you reach the first coffee break things are back on schedule — but only if you don't panic.

If you are acting as M.C. at a wedding reception and *the bride and groom are held up somewhere and are late arriving at their reception*, is there anything you can do? Why not tell the guests waiting for the arrival of the wedding party just what is happening? That way they will relax and not worry about what might have happened to the guests of honour. Perhaps there is a piano in the room and someone can play it. A little soft music can settle a restive crowd in minutes.

There will be other problems that are beyond the control of the M.C. *What happens if the guest speaker doesn't show up?* This sort of situation involves the whole organizing group. When did the speaker let you know that he wouldn't be able to make it? A day ahead? Two days ahead? The amount of warning time governs the possible course of action. If you have enough time, you might be able to arrange for a substitute. If there isn't time to arrange for a suitable substitute, don't crowd your luck. A hastily-recruited alternative speaker is being asked to do a great deal in a short space of time and under difficult circumstances. Everything may come together nicely and a new star be born, but don't count on it. If there is enough other business and entertainment connected with the program, why not explain things to the guests and forge ahead? At least everyone has a good meal and a night out.

There isn't room in this or any other chapter to consider all the things that might go wrong when you are acting as an M.C. The purpose of this book is to give you as much help as possible in seeing that things don't go wrong, and the purpose of this chapter is to let you know that even if something unexpected does crop up, there is a solution to the problem if you just *don't panic.*

To prevent panic, have you:

- told yourself that despite all your planning, something unexpected may arise?
- made a list of the office and home telephone numbers of program participants and included that list in your notes for the event?
- picked someone in attendance that you feel you could call upon quietly to make a telephone call or carry a message should the need arise?
- tucked a spare pen and a pad of paper into your information package in case you have to make a few notes?
- placed a few coins in your wallet in case someone has to make a telephone call from a pay phone?
- checked your information package and made sure that all your notes are in place?

CHAPTER X

On Wrapping It All Up

The evening is drawing to a close, and it looks as though all of the carefully-crafted pieces have fallen nicely into place. There is an air of comfortable excitement in the room, and you feel as though you have done a good job. While all of that may be true, there are a few loose ends that, when attended to, can make you not just a good M.C., but a great one.

Let's look at some of those odds and ends which the M.C. might look after. They are points which, for one reason or another, are not built into the plans you've put together with the organizers. The handling of the meal by the food service people is an example.

In many circumstances the meal will be catered on a voluntary basis or for a fee that goes towards the support of a worthy cause. Sometimes a group of people will undertake to cater for a function, donating their time and energy, and then use the money paid to them to further a cause in which they are interested. The mothers of a Junior A hockey team may handle a banquet as a way to raise funds for new team uniforms.

Why not thank those who prepared and served the food in a way that lets them know that their efforts were appreciated? It is a nice gesture to ask that the food-service staff step into the dining room for a minute before the crowd disperses or makes ready for a dance. The serving staff will probably come in from the kitchen area, cluster just in front of the swinging doors, and look a little embarrassed. Don't make too big a thing of it, but a few words along the lines of, "On behalf of all of us who enjoyed that delightful meal, thank you very much for the skill and care with which it was prepared and the speed and courtesy with which it was served. Again, from all of us, a sincere 'Thank you.'" Start the applause, the audience will follow, and the food-service people will feel appreciated.

Be prepared to make some sort of wrap-up comment to bring things to a conclusion. You'll have to wait and see how the circumstances develop before you decide what needs saying and how you are going to say it. You may find, as one example, that the dining-room staff are having a little trouble clearing the room of tables and the last of the coffee cups. In that situation, a quick trip back to the microphone and a comment such as, "Thank you very much for your kind attention, ladies and gentlemen. To assist the dining-room staff as they clear the tables and arrange things for the dance, would you be good enough to adjourn to the outer hall for just a few minutes? The music and dancing will begin in fifteen minutes."

You may find that the guests seem inclined to linger and chat with each other. If there is no pressing need for them to clear the room, and if the area and refreshments are still available, why not move back to your microphone and announce, "Thank you for your presence, ladies and gentlemen. There is no need to rush away now that the formal portion of our program is finished. The bar will remain open for another hour, and tea and coffee are available. Please stay and mingle with your friends and our special guests."

On the other hand, you may find that people are standing around and talking when you really would like them to call it an evening. Coupled with that is a program chairman who is telling you that he wished he had remembered to ask you to throw in a reminder about the next meeting. You can solve all the problems with an announcement such as, "Thank you, ladies and gentlemen. It has been a good evening, but that brings our program to a close. We look forward to seeing you all again at the next meeting of the group, which I'm sure you remember will be held on the evening of the third Thursday of next month.''

An announcement of this sort may not be necessary at all. But as M.C. you can keep an eye on the ebb and flow of the traffic and help to solve an unexpected and unplanned circumstance.

Once the crowd begins to disperse there are still a few things the M.C. can do, things that will be remembered and appreciated in the days and weeks to come.

Head-table guests, even though they may look completely calm and relaxed, are usually quite excited about the whole thing. You would be amazed at what they will leave behind at the head table in their excitement. After the guests have moved away from the head table, walk along behind their chairs and check to see if there are any eyeglasses, bits of jewelry, or wristwatches that have been left on the table and then become lost under a serviette or saucer.

One of the ladies may have found during the dinner that an earring had become uncomfortable. She may have slipped it off, put it on the table, and forgotten about it. Someone may have made a note or two on the back of the program and then left a favourite ballpoint pen beside a coffee cup in case he wanted to make another note. When the evening comes to a close, these personal items are forgotten in the confusion of handshaking and congratulations. Even if you aren't able to return all of these items to their owners immediately, you shouldn't have too much trouble tracking down these people the next day. They will appreciate your thoughtfulness.

Take a few minutes to look around the lectern. Are there any congratulatory telegrams that have been left in the shadows under the lectern? Once read, they may have been tucked away and forgotten. The recipients of the congratulations would probably like to have the originals for their scrapbooks.

Did the speaker leave his lecture notes on the lectern? At the conclusion of his talk he may have placed his notes on or under the lectern, intending to retrieve them later in the evening. But often people rushing up to ask questions or speak to the lecturer will distract him, and the notes that were intended to be preserved are left behind. Gather them up and see that they are passed on to their rightful owner. While the notes themselves may or may not be important, quite often there is reference material or clippings that would be hard to replace.

Walk along behind the chairs at the head table and check the backs of the chairs and the floor beneath the chairs and table. Scarves, handbags, glasses cases, and keys have a habit of slipping to the floor in all the excitement, and it is easier to get items like these back to their owners if you spot them before the tables and chairs are moved by the staff and while the people who dropped them aren't too far away.

Once you have checked the head table for lost-and-found items, do the same thing with the room in general and give your search a little thought as you move around. Is there a bouquet of flowers on the head table, a bouquet that is just going to be left behind? Perhaps the wife of the guest speaker would appreciate having it. Or there may be some other special guest in the gathering who might be recognized with a few flowers.

Have any documents or presentation items been left behind? Scrolls, framed long-service certificates, or other special gifts are often left behind. This doesn't reflect on the attitude of the recipients in any way. It is just that there is so much excitement going on around them that the presentation items slip from their minds just long enough to be left on a table or chair in all of the congratulatory handshaking that is going on.

The guest of honour would feel very badly if he were half-way home when he remembered that he had left his long-service certificate on his chair while he was being congratulated by the president and spouse. It is a nice touch if you can return the item quickly and quietly.

If the owners of these valuable items are not to be found quickly, see that the items themselves are placed in safekeeping somewhere so that they can be claimed or returned at a more appropriate time.

Are there any items that have been placed around the room by way of decoration, items that were brought or loaned just for the occasion? Sometimes old photographs, special documents, flags, ornaments, or ceremonial gavels are used to mark a special occasion. Make sure they are all looked after as the room is being cleared, lest they end up in a dusty lost-and-found box in a cloakroom somewhere.

As we have said so often before, in the minds of many people this sort of thing may not be seen as the responsibility of the M.C. On the other hand, someone has to do it, and it is a logical extension of the rôle you have played throughout the function. You have been mistress or master of the ceremonies, and this last exercise is a nice way to wrap it all up.

As the event draws to a conclusion, have you:

- decided whether the food service people should be thanked?
- if so, delegated someone to go to the kitchen area to ask them to come into the dining room for a moment?
- decided how you are going to word your "thank you" message?
- prepared a short paragraph or comment that will let the guests know that the formal proceedings are over and suggest what they might do next?
- checked the lectern, head table, and dining area for forgotten personal items and arranged for the return of any you find?
- checked the head table and dining area for special items that should be removed for safekeeping?

CHAPTER XI

After the Ball is Over

Meredith Willson led off his autobiography with a delightful story that just might touch the heart and feelings of the M.C. as the big event draws to a successful close.

Meredith Willson, the accomplished musician and orchestra leader, claims that the story was passed on to him by an old Moravian flute player. My recollection of the story is as follows:

> Once upon a time I was a member of a small orchestra, and we played all over my country, wherever we could find an audience. We were very good, and our fame spread throughout the land. Soon we were invited to the royal court to play before the king. When we had finished our performance, the king was so pleased that he instructed the court treasurer to take us to the counting house where, he said, we could each fill our instrument with as much gold as that instrument could carry. Within minutes, the tuba player was struggling out the door of the counting house, the bell of his tuba filled with gold coins. The trombone player had stuffed as many pieces of gold into his horn as it could possibly carry. The trumpet player, too, had filled the bell of his horn with gold.
>
> And there I stood with my piccolo.

Meredith Willson titled his autobiography *And There I Stood With My Piccolo*, very possibly echoing the feelings of the typical M.C. at the end of an evening.

The graduates are busy being photographed and fussed over. The retirees are being congratulated. Friends are exclaiming over the awards that have been presented to the long-service employees. The bride and groom are being hugged and sent on their way with the best wishes. There are people lined up six deep to shake the hand of the guest speaker and ask interesting questions.

And there you stand with your piccolo.

But just like the Moravian flute player, you have been part of a group that produced beautiful music. You have helped to bring excitement and joy to all of these people. You have sent them on their way with warm, happy memories that will last them through years to come.

And that's not a bad reward for an evening's work, now is it?

Names You Will Need

Numbers You Will Need

Special Equipment You Will Need

_____

_____

_____

_____

_____

_____

_____

_____

_____

_____

_____

_____

_____

Toasts, Talkers, Titles & Times

Questions to Be Answered

_____

_____

_____

_____

_____

_____

_____

_____

_____

_____

_____

_____

_____

_____

_____

_____

General Notes

About the Author

Born in Edmonton, Alex Mair graduated from the University of Alberta with a degree in Civil Engineering. For nearly twenty years he worked in a variety of areas related to engineering. He began to write and narrate for the CBC in the early 1960s, launched the Radio and Television Arts course at the Northern Alberta Institute of Technology in Edmonton, and wrote a column for the *Edmonton Journal* for several years.

Mair continues to live in Edmonton and divides his time between writing and speaking engagements. He is the author of the recent book, *How to Speak in Public*.

Editor / Nancy Marcotte
Designer / David Shaw
Cover Illustration / James Kempkes
Photographer / Michael Cohen
Typesetter / Accurate Typesetting Ltd.
Manufacturer / Friesen Printers
